SECRETS TO REACH YOUR GOALS WITH POSITIVITY

STRATEGIES FOR ACHIEVING YOUR DREAMS

DR. JAGADEESH PILLAI

Made with ♥ on the Notion Press Platform
www.notionpress.com

|| Dedicated to all wisdom seekers around the World ||

॰॰

Contents

Contents

Prayer

**"Om Bhadram Karnebhih Shrunuyaama
DevaahBhadram Pashyemaakshabhiryajatraah
SthirairangaistushtuvaamsastanoobhihVyashema
Devahitam YadaayuhSwasti Na Indro
VridhashravaahSwasti Nah Pooshaa
VishwavedaahSwasti Nastaarkshyo ArishtanemihSwasti
No Brihaspatir DadhaatuOm Shantih, Shantih, Shantih"**

The literal meaning of this mantra is: OM. O Gods! Let us
hear auspicious words from our ears. O reverent Gods! Let
us behold propitious visions from our eyes, let our organs
and body be stable, healthy, and strong. Let us do that
which is pleasing to the gods in the life span allotted to us.
May Indra, inscribed in the scriptures, bring us fortune!
May Pushan, the knower of the world, grant us prosperity!
May Trakshya, who vanquishes enemies, bestow us with
blessings! May Brihaspati bring us success!
OM Peace, Peace, Peace.

About The Author

Dr. Jagadeesh Pillai is a renowned Guinness World Record holder, writer, and researcher hailing from Varanasi, also known as the abode of Lord Shiva. With a Ph.D. in Vedic Science and a range of creative ideas and achievements, he is a true polymath. He is the author of more than 100 books including Research Publications. Although his roots can be traced back to Kerala, the people of Varanasi hold him in high regard and affectionately consider him one of their own.

In 1998, Dr. Pillai was offered a job at Banaras Hindu University, but he left the position after only two months to pursue greater goals in life. He believed that in order to study Indian scriptures and engage in other creative endeavours, he needed to retire from the daily grind of working solely for money at a young age.

He started an export business from scratch, using the knowledge he had gained from a previous job in the industry. His intelligence and unique approach to business led to great success in a short period of time, earning him more in just a decade and a half than he would have in a lifetime working in a government job. Upon the passing of Dr. APJ Abdul Kalam, Dr. Pillai decided to leave the business and dedicate himself to reading, studying, researching, and experimenting.

During his tenure in the export business, Dr. Pillai traveled to over 16 countries, gaining valuable insight and experiencing the world and life in detail.

Dr. Pillai has achieved four Guinness World Records in the following subjects:

"Script to Screen" - In this record, Dr. Pillai produced and directed an animation film within the shortest time possible, breaking the previous record set by Canadians. He has also received numerous national and international awards and recognitions for this achievement.

Longest Line of Postcards - For this record, Dr. Pillai created a line of 16,300 postcards on the occasion of the 163rd anniversary of Indian Postal Day. The event also included a questionnaire about the Indian flag.

Largest Poster Awareness Campaign - Dr. Pillai designed an awareness campaign on the subject of "Beti Bachao - Beti Padhao" (Save the Girl Child - Educate the Girl Child) to achieve this record.

Largest Envelope - In tribute to the Indian Prime Minister's "Make in India" initiative, Dr. Pillai created a 4000 square meter envelope using waste paper to achieve this record.

Attempted - **70000 Candles on a 210 kg Cake** - To celebrate the 70th Indian Independence Day, Dr. Pillai attempted to light 70,000 candles on a 210 kg cake, which was recorded in World Records India.

Attempted - **Documentary on Dhamek Stupa of Sarnath in 17 Languages** - Dr. Pillai attempted to create a documentary on the Dhamek Stupa of Sarnath, dubbing it in 17 different languages. The result of this attempt is currently awaiting confirmation from the Guinness World Records.

Dr. Pillai is skilled in teaching the Bhagavad Gita, a Hindu scripture, and is popular among young people. He has helped many young people improve their lives through his motivational teachings.

In addition to teaching, he has composed and sung numerous Sanskrit Bhajans and patriotic songs.

He has also written and directed several short films and documentaries for awareness campaigns, and has volunteered with the police in both UP and Kerala to spread awareness about various issues through videos and photography.

Incredibly, he has produced and directed over 100 documentaries about the city of Varanasi, all on his own.

He has also helped and guided more than 25 boys and girls to achieve world records through creative and innovative methods. He is a multifaceted person who uses his intellect and the blessings given to him by God to excel in various areas. He is both a teacher and a student, always learning and teaching, and is able to master any subject he comes across.

He is a selfless social activist and motivational speaker who has overcome struggles and failures to become a successful and enthusiastic individual with a rich life experience.

In addition to his work with the Bhagavad Gita, he is also an efficient Tarot card reader, Astro-Vastu consultant, and a talented singer and composer. He has sung the entire Ram Charita Manas and Bhagavad Gita in his own compositions, and has sung the phrase "Lokah Samastha Sukhino Bhavantu" in 50 different languages. He is currently working on a detailed and scientific study of Vedas, Upanishads, Puranas, and the Bhagavad Gita. He has also composed and sung the Hanuman Chalisa and Gayatri Mantra in 108 and 1008 different compositions, respectively.

Awards - Four Times Guinness World Records, Winner of Mahatma Gandhi Vishwa Shanti Puraskar, Mahatma Gandhi Global Peace Ambassador, Kashi Ratna Award, Dr. APJ Abdul Kalam Motivational Person of the Year 2017, Mother Teresa Award, Indira Gandhi Priyadarshini Award, Bharat Vikas Ratna Award, Udyog Ratna Award, Vigyan Prasar Award, Poorvanchal Ratn Samman.

Preface

Welcome to "Secrets to Reach Your Goals with Positivity: Strategies for Achieving Your Dreams." This book has been written with the aim of guiding and inspiring you on your journey to achieve your goals with positivity.

We all have dreams and aspirations, but sometimes it can be difficult to turn those dreams into a reality. Obstacles and setbacks can arise, causing us to feel discouraged and unmotivated. It is during these moments that the power of positivity becomes especially important.

In this book, we will explore the various strategies and techniques that you can use to cultivate a positive mindset and maintain a strong level of motivation as you work towards your goals. We will cover topics such as managing emotions, building resilience, overcoming procrastination, developing self-esteem, finding your passions, and much more.

With the help of these strategies, you will be equipped with the tools and mindset needed to stay motivated and focused, even in the face of challenges. By combining positivity with persistence, determination, and a support system, you will be able to achieve your goals and live the life of your dreams.

We hope that this book will serve as a source of inspiration and encouragement, helping you to stay positive and motivated as you work towards your goals. With the right attitude and approach, anything is possible. Let's get started!

I

Understanding the Power of Positivity and its Impact on Achieving Goals

Many people struggle to reach their goals because they focus on the obstacles and difficulties that stand in their way, rather than the opportunities and solutions that can help them achieve their dreams. Positivity, on the other hand, involves focusing on the good things in life, cultivating a positive attitude, and surrounding oneself with positive influences. This can have a profound effect on our ability to achieve our goals and live a fulfilling life.

One of the key benefits of positivity is increased motivation. When we have a positive outlook, we are more likely to see challenges as opportunities, rather than obstacles. This can give us the drive and energy we need to pursue our goals with determination and confidence. Positivity also helps us to maintain our focus and stay motivated, even when faced with setbacks or difficulties. It can be easy to become discouraged and give up when faced with challenges, but a positive outlook can help us to persevere and keep moving forward.

Another important benefit of positivity is improved mental and emotional well-being. When we focus on the positive, we are more likely to feel happy, confident, and fulfilled. This can lead to better physical health and improved relationships, both of which are critical to achieving our goals. Additionally, positivity can help us to reduce stress, anxiety, and depression, which can be major roadblocks to success.

Finally, positivity can help us to build stronger relationships and networks of support. When we are positive and optimistic, we are more likely to attract positive and supportive people into our lives, and this can be invaluable as we work towards our goals. Having a strong network of friends, family members, and colleagues who believe in us and support us can make all the difference when it comes to achieving our dreams.

In this book, we will explore the power of positivity and provide strategies for cultivating a positive attitude, building positive relationships, and maintaining a positive outlook, even in the face of challenges and setbacks. We will also explore how positivity can help us to overcome obstacles and reach our goals, both personally and professionally.

In conclusion, understanding the power of positivity and its impact on achieving goals is a critical step towards reaching your full potential. By cultivating a positive outlook, building supportive relationships, and focusing on the good things in life, you can transform your life and achieve your goals with ease and confidence.

"The power of positivity is not just a force to be reckoned with, it's a force that can change the world."

৪৩

II

Establishing Clear and Measurable Objectives

In order to reach your goals with positivity, it is essential to establish clear and measurable objectives. This means taking the time to define your goals in a specific and actionable way, so that you can track your progress and stay motivated as you work towards your dreams.

One of the key principles of setting clear and measurable objectives is specificity. Rather than simply stating that you want to "be happy" or "earn more money," you should define your goals in specific, concrete terms. For example, instead of saying that you want to be happy, you might set a goal to "spend 30 minutes each day practicing gratitude," or to "meditate for 10 minutes each morning." Similarly, instead of saying that you want to earn more money, you might set a goal to "increase your income by 10% in the next 12 months," or to "save $500 per month for the next 6 months."

Another important aspect of setting clear and measurable objectives is to make sure that your goals are achievable. This means setting goals that are challenging, but not unrealistic. It is important to take into account your current level of skill and experience, as well as any external factors that may impact your ability to reach your goals. By setting achievable goals, you will be more likely to stay motivated and confident, even in the face of setbacks or obstacles.

Finally, it is essential to set goals that are measurable. This means creating goals that can be tracked and quantified. For example, instead of setting a goal to "be more productive," you might set a goal to "complete 5 tasks from your to-do list each day." This type of goal is much easier to track and measure, and will help you to stay focused and motivated as you work towards your dreams.

In conclusion, establishing clear and measurable objectives is a critical step towards reaching your goals with positivity. By taking the time to define your goals in specific, achievable, and measurable terms, you will be able to track your progress and stay motivated as you work towards your dreams. Throughout this book, we will provide strategies and tools to help you establish clear and measurable objectives, so that you can reach your goals with ease and confidence.

*"Positive thoughts lead to positive actions,
and positive actions lead to positive results."*

⚮

III

Building a Positive Mindset and Overcoming Negative Thinking

Building a positive mindset and overcoming negative thinking is an essential component of reaching your goals with positivity. Negative thoughts and self-doubt can undermine your confidence and motivation, making it difficult to achieve your goals. On the other hand, a positive mindset can help you to stay motivated and confident, even in the face of obstacles and setbacks.

One of the key strategies for building a positive mindset is to practice gratitude. Gratitude involves taking the time to focus on the good things in your life, rather than dwelling on what you lack or what is going wrong. By focusing on the positive, you can cultivate a more positive outlook and feel more fulfilled and happy. You might try writing a daily gratitude journal, in which you reflect on the things you are grateful for each day. You can also try saying affirmations, which are positive statements that help to reinforce your positive outlook and boost your self-confidence.

Another important strategy for building a positive mindset is to surround yourself with positive influences. This means surrounding yourself with people who uplift and support you, and limiting your exposure to negative influences like toxic friends, negative media, and pessimistic co-workers. By surrounding yourself with positive people and experiences, you can build a more positive outlook and feel more confident and motivated as you work towards your goals.

It is also important to recognize and challenge negative thoughts and self-doubt. When we are feeling negative, it can be easy to fall into a pattern of negative thinking, in which we focus on what is going wrong and dwell on our shortcomings. However, these thoughts are often not based in reality, and can hold us back from achieving our goals. To overcome negative thinking, you can try practicing mindfulness, which involves paying attention to your thoughts and feelings in the present moment. By becoming aware of your negative thoughts, you can challenge them and replace them with more positive, constructive thoughts.

In conclusion, building a positive mindset and overcoming negative thinking is a critical step towards reaching your goals with positivity. By focusing on gratitude, surrounding yourself with positive influences, and challenging negative thoughts, you can cultivate a more positive outlook and stay motivated and confident as you work towards your dreams. Throughout this book, we will provide strategies and tools to help you build a positive mindset, so that you can reach your goals with ease and confidence.

"The greatest barrier to success is not the absence of ability, but the absence of determination."

❧

IV

Managing Emotions and Staying Focused

Managing emotions and staying focused are critical components of reaching your goals with positivity. Emotions like stress, anxiety, and frustration can undermine your confidence and motivation, making it difficult to stay focused and achieve your goals. On the other hand, being able to manage your emotions and maintain focus can help you to stay motivated and confident, even in the face of obstacles and setbacks. One of the key strategies for managing emotions and staying focused is to practice mindfulness.

Mindfulness is the practice of paying attention to your thoughts, feelings, and experiences in the present moment, without judgment. By practicing mindfulness, you can learn to stay calm and centered, even in the face of stress and anxiety. You might try incorporating mindfulness into your daily routine, by taking a few minutes each day to simply focus on your breath, or by participating in a mindfulness meditation. Another important strategy for managing emotions and staying focused is to prioritize self-care. This includes taking care of your physical and emotional well-being by engaging in activities like exercise, eating well, and getting enough sleep. It also means taking time for self-reflection and self-compassion, and learning to recognize and manage negative self-talk.

It's also helpful to cultivate a growth mindset, which means focusing on learning and personal development, rather than being fixated on outcome or failure. When you have a growth mindset, you're more likely to be resilient in the face of challenges, and to see setbacks as opportunities for growth and improvement.

Finally, it's important to identify and challenge negative thought patterns and limiting beliefs. This can involve questioning your negative thoughts and replacing them with more positive and supportive ones. It can also mean seeking out new experiences and learning new skills, to broaden your perspective and expand your belief system.

In summary, managing emotions and staying focused require a combination of mindfulness, self-care, a growth mindset, and challenging negative thought patterns. By incorporating these strategies into your daily routine, you can build the emotional intelligence and resilience you need to reach your goals with positivity.

"Gratitude is the key to unlocking a positive mindset and the door to a fulfilling life."

৪৩

V

Building Resilience and Coping with Setbacks

Reaching your goals can be a long and challenging journey, and setbacks and failures are an inevitable part of the process. However, the way you respond to setbacks can make all the difference in determining your success. Building resilience and learning to cope with setbacks is crucial to achieving your goals with positivity.

One of the key components of resilience is having a growth mindset. This means recognizing that failures and setbacks are opportunities for growth and learning, rather than permanent roadblocks. When you have a growth mindset, you're more likely to bounce back from setbacks and persist in pursuing your goals, even in the face of challenges.

It's also important to cultivate a positive self-image and a sense of self-worth that is not tied to your achievements or failures. By accepting and loving yourself, regardless of your successes or failures, you'll be better equipped to handle the ups and downs of the journey towards your goals.

Another strategy for building resilience is to develop a strong support system. This can include friends, family, mentors, and a community of like-minded individuals who will encourage and support you, even in the face of setbacks.

In addition to having a strong support system, it's also important to engage in self-care and stress management. This includes regular exercise, healthy eating, getting enough sleep, and taking time to relax and recharge.

Finally, learning effective coping strategies can help you to manage the stress and emotions that often accompany setbacks. This may include practicing mindfulness and self-compassion, seeking out professional support, and finding healthy ways to express and manage your emotions.

In summary, building resilience and coping with setbacks require a combination of a growth mindset, self-care and stress management, a strong support system, and effective coping strategies. By developing these skills and practices, you'll be better equipped to handle the challenges that come your way, and to achieve your goals with positivity and resilience.

"Believe in yourself, and all that you are.
Know that there is something inside you that
is greater than any obstacle."

ॐ

VI

The Power of Positive Affirmations and Visualization

Positive affirmations and visualization are powerful tools for building resilience and reaching your goals with positivity. Positive affirmations are short, positive statements that you repeat to yourself, designed to help you focus on your strengths, build confidence, and counteract negative self-talk.

Visualization involves using your imagination to create mental images of your desired outcome. By visualizing yourself achieving your goals, you can train your mind to focus on the positive, and build the confidence and motivation you need to make your goals a reality.

When used together, positive affirmations and visualization can help you to overcome obstacles, stay motivated, and build the resilience you need to reach your goals. For example, you can use positive affirmations to reinforce your belief in yourself, and visualization to see yourself overcoming challenges and achieving your goals.

It's important to make positive affirmations and visualization a regular part of your daily routine. This can be as simple as taking a few minutes each day to repeat positive affirmations to yourself, and visualizing your desired outcome.

In addition to being a powerful tool for building resilience and motivation, positive affirmations and visualization can also help you to develop a growth mindset, cultivate a positive self-image, and overcome limiting beliefs.

In summary, the power of positive affirmations and visualization lies in their ability to help you to focus on the positive, build resilience, and achieve your goals with positivity. By making these practices a regular part of your routine, you'll be well on your way to reaching your goals with confidence and determination.

"*Don't wait for opportunities, create them.*"

ॐ

VII

Building a Support System and Connecting with Others

Building a strong support system and connecting with others can be a key factor in achieving your goals with positivity. Having a network of supportive individuals can provide you with encouragement, motivation, and a sense of belonging, all of which can help you to stay focused and overcome obstacles.

One of the first steps in building a support system is to identify the people in your life who are most likely to be supportive of your goals. This might include friends, family members, coworkers, or members of a community or organization that shares your interests.

Once you've identified potential supporters, the next step is to reach out and connect with them. This might involve asking for advice, sharing your goals, or simply spending time with them on a regular basis.

In addition to building a network of supportive individuals, it can also be helpful to participate in a group or community that shares your interests. This can provide you with a sense of belonging, and offer opportunities to connect with like-minded individuals who can provide support and encouragement.

It's also important to cultivate a positive and supportive inner dialogue, and to practice self-compassion and self-care. By treating yourself with kindness and understanding, you can build the confidence and resilience you need to overcome setbacks and pursue your goals with positivity.

Finally, don't be afraid to seek out professional support if you need it. This might include working with a coach, a therapist, or a mentor who can provide guidance and support as you work towards your goals.

In summary, building a support system and connecting with others is a critical component of achieving your goals with positivity. By cultivating a network of supportive individuals, participating in a group or community, and seeking out professional support when needed, you'll be better equipped to handle the challenges that come your way, and to reach your goals with resilience and determination.

"Success is not final, failure is not fatal: it is
the courage to continue that counts."

৪৩

VIII

Overcoming Procrastination and Staying Motivated

Procrastination and a lack of motivation can be major obstacles to reaching your goals. These challenges can leave you feeling stuck and prevent you from making progress towards your desired outcome.

However, by taking a proactive approach and developing strategies to overcome procrastination and stay motivated, you can achieve your goals with positivity and determination.

One of the key strategies for overcoming procrastination is to set clear and achievable goals. This involves breaking your larger goal down into smaller, more manageable tasks, and establishing deadlines for each. This will help you to stay focused and avoid feeling overwhelmed by the bigger picture.

Another important strategy for overcoming procrastination is to establish a routine and stick to it. This might involve setting aside specific times each day for working on your goals, and limiting distractions and interruptions during these times.

It's also important to cultivate a growth mindset and focus on progress, rather than perfection. This involves recognizing that setbacks and obstacles are a natural part of the process, and that success is often the result of many small steps, rather than one big leap.

To stay motivated, it's also important to identify your values and connect your goals to your larger life purpose. This will help you to maintain focus and find meaning and fulfillment in the pursuit of your goals.

Finally, be sure to take care of yourself and practice self-compassion and self-care. By prioritizing your well-being and treating yourself with kindness and understanding, you'll be better equipped to handle the ups and downs of the journey, and to maintain your motivation and focus.

In summary, overcoming procrastination and staying motivated are critical components of reaching your goals with positivity. By setting clear goals, establishing a routine, cultivating a growth mindset, and taking care of yourself, you'll be well on your way to achieving your dreams with confidence and determination.

"Embrace change, it's the only constant in life."

ೞ

IX

Understanding and Managing Perfectionism

Perfectionism can be a double-edged sword, as it can drive you to strive for excellence, but also hold you back from reaching your full potential. On one hand, striving for excellence can be a valuable and motivating factor in achieving your goals, but on the other hand, perfectionism can also lead to feelings of inadequacy, anxiety, and disappointment.

To reach your goals with positivity, it's important to understand the nature of perfectionism, and to develop strategies for managing it in a healthy and effective way.

One of the key strategies for managing perfectionism is to understand that perfection is an unrealistic standard, and to focus on progress, rather than perfection. This involves accepting that setbacks and obstacles are a natural part of the journey, and that success is often the result of many small steps, rather than one big leap.

Another important strategy is to cultivate a growth mindset and embrace challenges as opportunities for learning and growth. By recognizing that failures and setbacks are not evidence of your worth or abilities, you can increase your resilience and reduce your stress and anxiety.

It's also important to set realistic goals, and to recognize that it's okay to make mistakes. By setting achievable and flexible goals, you can reduce the pressure to be perfect, and allow yourself the freedom to grow and learn at your own pace.

Finally, it's important to engage in self-care and self-compassion, and to recognize that you're not alone. By taking care of yourself and connecting with others, you'll be better equipped to manage feelings of anxiety and inadequacy, and to maintain your focus and motivation.

In conclusion, understanding and managing perfectionism is a critical component of reaching your goals with positivity. By embracing a growth mindset, focusing on progress, setting realistic goals, and taking care of yourself, you'll be well on your way to achieving your dreams with confidence and determination.

"Confidence comes from within, not from external validation."

X

The Role of Gratitude and Mindfulness in Positivity

Gratitude and mindfulness are powerful tools for cultivating positivity and achieving your goals. Both practices have been shown to have a profound impact on mental and emotional well-being, helping to reduce stress, increase happiness, and boost resilience.

Gratitude involves recognizing and appreciating the good things in your life, and can be cultivated by taking time each day to reflect on the things you're thankful for. Practicing gratitude can help to shift your focus away from negative thoughts and experiences, and increase your sense of well-being.

Mindfulness, on the other hand, involves paying attention to the present moment, without judgment. By practicing mindfulness, you can increase your self-awareness and reduce stress and anxiety, as well as improve your focus and motivation.

Both gratitude and mindfulness can help you to maintain a positive outlook and stay motivated, even in the face of setbacks and obstacles. When you cultivate a sense of gratitude and mindfulness, you'll be better equipped to handle stress, overcome challenges, and achieve your goals with positivity.

Incorporating gratitude and mindfulness into your daily routine can be simple and straightforward. You might try starting each day with a gratitude journal, in which you write down a few things you're thankful for. You could also practice mindfulness meditation, or simply take a few minutes each day to focus on your breath and be present in the moment.

In conclusion, gratitude and mindfulness are key components of reaching your goals with positivity. By incorporating these practices into your daily routine, you'll be better equipped to handle stress, overcome obstacles, and maintain your focus and motivation, helping you to achieve your dreams with confidence and determination.

*"Every setback is an opportunity to grow,
learn and become better."*

☙

XI

Building Self-Esteem and Confidence

Self-esteem and confidence are critical components of reaching your goals with positivity. When you have high levels of self-esteem and confidence, you're more likely to feel motivated and capable of overcoming obstacles and setbacks. On the other hand, low self-esteem and confidence can make it difficult to stay motivated and achieve your goals, leading to feelings of self-doubt and insecurity.

Building self-esteem and confidence involves taking a proactive approach to your thoughts and feelings, and learning to recognize and challenge negative self-talk. You might start by taking an inventory of your thoughts and feelings, and noting any negative or self-critical messages that arise. Then, you can work to challenge these negative messages by reframing them in a more positive light, and replacing them with more supportive and encouraging thoughts.

In addition to challenging negative self-talk, there are other strategies you can use to build self-esteem and confidence, including:

Setting achievable goals: When you set and achieve small, manageable goals, you'll feel a sense of accomplishment and confidence, helping to build your self-esteem over time.

Practicing self-care: Taking care of your physical and emotional health can help to boost your self-esteem and confidence, making you feel more capable and resilient.

Surrounding yourself with positive and supportive people: Being around people who believe in you and support your goals can help to build your self-esteem and confidence, making it easier to stay motivated and focused.

Celebrating your successes: Taking time to acknowledge and celebrate your successes, no matter how small, can help to boost your self-esteem and confidence, and keep you motivated and focused on your goals.

Building self-esteem and confidence takes time and effort, but with persistence and determination, you can learn to recognize and challenge negative self-talk, set achievable goals, and celebrate your successes, helping you to reach your goals with positivity and confidence.

In conclusion, self-esteem and confidence play a critical

role in helping you to achieve your goals with positivity. By taking a proactive approach to your thoughts and feelings, and incorporating strategies like goal setting, self-care, positive relationships, and celebrating your successes, you'll be better equipped to build your self-esteem and confidence, and achieve your dreams with determination and resilience.

"Your mindset is the foundation upon which all success is built."

XII

Finding and Pursuing Your Passions

Finding and pursuing your passions can be one of the most fulfilling and motivating experiences of your life. When you're passionate about what you're doing, it's easier to stay focused and motivated, and to overcome obstacles and setbacks. In order to reach your goals with positivity, it's important to find and pursue your passions, and to use that drive and motivation to help you achieve your dreams.

One of the keys to finding and pursuing your passions is to explore your interests and identify what truly excites you. You might start by trying new things, such as taking a class or volunteering in a new area, to see what captures your imagination and interests. Another strategy is to reflect on your strengths and skills, and consider how you might use those skills in a job or hobby that you're passionate about.

Once you've identified your passions, it's important to make a plan for pursuing them. This might involve setting achievable goals and taking small steps toward your passions, such as taking a class, volunteering, or starting a side hustle. You might also consider seeking out supportive friends, family members, or a mentor who can help you stay motivated and focused on your goals.

It's also important to be flexible and open to change. Your passions may evolve over time, and it's okay to pivot and try new things if you find that your interests have shifted. The key is to stay true to yourself and to be open to new experiences and opportunities that may arise.

Finally, it's important to maintain a positive and optimistic outlook. When you're pursuing your passions, you're likely to face obstacles and setbacks, but it's important to stay focused and motivated, and to believe in yourself and your abilities. Surround yourself with positive and supportive people, and stay committed to your goals, even when the going gets tough.

In conclusion, finding and pursuing your passions is a critical component of reaching your goals with positivity. By exploring your interests, setting achievable goals, seeking support, staying flexible and open to change, and maintaining a positive outlook, you'll be better equipped to achieve your goals and live a fulfilling life filled with passion and purpose.

"*Happiness is not a destination, it's a journey.*"

XIII

Learning to Adapt and Be Flexible

In today's fast-paced and constantly changing world, it's more important than ever to be adaptable and flexible. The ability to adjust to new situations and to pivot when necessary is key to achieving your goals with positivity. By learning to adapt and be flexible, you'll be better equipped to overcome obstacles and to stay motivated and focused, even in the face of change and uncertainty.

One of the keys to adapting and being flexible is to remain open-minded and willing to consider new ideas and approaches. This might involve stepping outside of your comfort zone, seeking out new experiences and opportunities, and being willing to learn from your mistakes and failures.

Another important strategy is to maintain a growth mindset, and to approach challenges as opportunities for growth and learning. This means embracing change and uncertainty, and being willing to experiment and try new things, even if they may be outside of your comfort zone.

It's also important to develop strong problem-solving skills and to be able to think creatively and outside of the box. When faced with obstacles, it's important to be able to identify potential solutions and to take action to overcome the challenge. This might involve seeking out help from others, such as friends, family members, or a mentor, or seeking out resources and tools that can help you to overcome the obstacle.

Another key aspect of adaptability is resilience. It's important to be able to bounce back from setbacks and to maintain a positive outlook, even when things don't go as planned. This might involve practicing self-care, seeking support from others, and being willing to take time to recharge and refocus when necessary.

Finally, it's important to be proactive and to take steps to prepare for change and uncertainty. This might involve developing a contingency plan, seeking out resources and support, and staying informed about trends and developments in your field or industry.

In conclusion, learning to adapt and be flexible is an essential component of reaching your goals with positivity. By remaining open-minded, embracing change, developing strong problem-solving skills, being resilient, and taking proactive steps to prepare for uncertainty, you'll be better equipped to overcome obstacles and to stay motivated and focused on your goals.

"The secret to achieving your goals is not just hard work, but smart work and positive thinking."

☙

XIV

The Power of Persistence and Determination

Reaching your goals with positivity is a journey, not a destination. Along the way, you will encounter obstacles, setbacks, and challenges. It is how you react to these obstacles that will determine your success. This is where persistence and determination come into play.

Persistence is the ability to keep going, even in the face of difficulties. It is the drive to keep pushing forward, no matter what. When you are persistent, you are not easily discouraged and you refuse to give up. Determination is the resolve to achieve your goals, no matter what it takes. It is the unwavering commitment to see things through to the end.

Together, persistence and determination give you the

strength to overcome obstacles, stay focused, and reach your goals. They help you to keep pushing forward, even when the road ahead is difficult.

One of the keys to building persistence and determination is to have a clear vision of what you want to achieve. When you have a clear vision, it is easier to stay focused and motivated, even in the face of setbacks. Additionally, having a clear vision helps you to prioritize your efforts and stay on track, even when you are feeling overwhelmed.

Another important factor in building persistence and determination is having a growth mindset. This is the belief that you can grow, change, and improve over time. When you have a growth mindset, you approach challenges as opportunities to learn and grow, rather than as obstacles to be avoided. This helps you to maintain a positive attitude, even in the face of difficulty.

Finally, surrounding yourself with supportive and encouraging people is another key to building persistence and determination. When you have a supportive network, you are more likely to stay motivated and focused, even in the face of challenges. Surrounding yourself with people who believe in you and support your goals can help you to stay positive and motivated, even in the face of setbacks.

In conclusion, persistence and determination are essential components of reaching your goals with positivity. By having a clear vision, a growth mindset, and a supportive network, you can build the resilience and determination you need to overcome obstacles, stay focused, and achieve your dreams.

"Be persistent, determination is the key to unlocking your potential."

৪৩

XV

Achieving Your Goals with Positivity

In this book, we have explored the key strategies for reaching your goals with positivity. We have discussed the importance of managing emotions, building resilience, and staying motivated, as well as the role of positive affirmations, visualization, gratitude, mindfulness, self-esteem, confidence, passions, adaptability, persistence, and determination.

It's now time to bring all of these strategies together and use them to achieve your goals with positivity. The key to success is to find what works best for you and to tailor these strategies to meet your individual needs. No two people are exactly alike, and what works for one person may not work for another. However, by being open-minded and flexible, you can find the strategies that work best for you and use them to reach your goals with confidence and positivity.

One of the most important things to remember is that success takes time and effort. You will encounter setbacks and obstacles along the way, but it's important to stay focused and persist in your efforts. Building resilience and coping with setbacks will help you to stay positive and motivated, even in the face of adversity.

By combining all of these strategies, you can create a powerful formula for success. You can use positive affirmations and visualization to build self-esteem and confidence, practice gratitude and mindfulness to stay centered and focused, and find and pursue your passions to stay motivated and inspired. And by being persistent and determined, you can overcome obstacles and achieve your goals with positivity.

In conclusion, reaching your goals with positivity is a journey that requires effort and dedication. By incorporating the strategies outlined in this book into your daily routine, you can create a positive and empowering mindset that will help you to achieve your dreams and reach your goals with confidence and determination.

"The most important investment you can make is in yourself."

৪৩

OTHER BOOKS OF THE AUTHOR

1. The Moments When I Met God
2. Kashiyile Theertha Pathangal
3. Guru Gyan Vani
4. Abhiprerak Gita
5. Assi Se Jain Ghat Tak
6. Hopelessness Of Arjuna
7. The Soul And It's True Nature
8. Sense Of Action (Karma)
9. Action Through Wisdom
10. Action Through Wisdom
11. Theory And Practical Of Every Action
12. Logical Understanding Of The Supreme
13. The Imperishable Supreme
14. Yatra Nishadraj Se Hanuman Ghat Tak
15. Yatra Karnatak Ghat Se Raja Ghat Tak
16. Yatra Pandey Ghat Se Prayagraj Ghat Tak
17. Yatra Ranjendra Prasad Ghat Se Dattatreya Ghat Tak
18. Yaatrasindhiya Ghat Se Gwaliar Ghat Tak
19. Yatra Mangala Gauri Ghat Se Hanuman Gadhi Ghat Tak
20. Yatra Gaay Ghat Se Nishad Ghat Tak
21. Maa Ganga, Ghaten Evm Utsav
22. Ganga Arti Dev Deepavali Evam Any Utsav
23. Potentials Of Digitalized India
24. Vedic Consciousness
25. A Brief Introduction To Vedic Science
26. Kashi Ke Barah Jyotirling
27. Impact Of Motivation
28. Let's Have A Milky Way Journey
29. Color Therapy In A Nutshell

OTHER BOOKS OF THE AUTHOR

30. Rigveda In A Nutshell
31. Yajurveda In A Nutshell
32. Samveda In A Nutshell
33. Atharva Veda In A Nutshell
34. Ayushman Bhava - Ayurveda
35. Srimad Bhagavad Gita And Upanishad Connection
36. Srimad Bhagavad Gita - An Attempt To Summarize Each Chapter.
37. Facts And Impact Of Nakshatra
38. Astro Gems - Navaratna
39. Ekadashi - A Concise Overview
40. A Concise View Of Hanuman Chalisa
41. Inspirational Gita
42. Nakshatraranyam
43. Summary Of 18 Mahapuranas
44. Synopsis Of 18 Upa Puranas
45. Rigvediya Upanishads
46. Shukla Yajurvediya Upanishads
47. Krishna Yajurvediya Upanishads
48. Samavediya Upanishads
49. Atharvavediya Upanishads
50. The Seven Great Sages
51. From Rocket Scientist To President Dr. Apj Abdul Kalam
52. The Visionary's Voice - Quotes Of Dr. Apj Abdul Kalam
53. The Wisdom Of Swami Vivekananda: Insights And Inspiration From A Legendary Spiritual Teacher
54. Ayurvedic Remedies From The Garden
55. Sages And Seers
56. Rising Strong – Motivational Stories Of Women
57. Beyond Flames -Mystery Stories Of Funeral Ghat Manikarnika
58. The Origins Of Tulsi: A Look At The Mythological Roots Of The Plant"

90. Astrological Remedies
91. The Secret Power Of Motivation
92. Secret Of Developing Your Inner Strength
93. The Secret Path To Motivation
94. The Art And Secret Of Positive Thinking
95. The Secrets Of Practicing Ethical Living
96. Indian Art And Painting
97. The Indian Herbalism
98. Bharatanatyam To Kathak
99. Exploring India's Astrological Remedies
100. The Indian Festival Of Flowers
101. Indian Handicrafts
102. The Splashes Of Joy – India's Colour Festival
103. The Indian Science Of Astrology
104. The Indian Mythology
105. Path To Enlightenment
106. The Indian Spirituality For Children
107. Aromas Of India
108. The Secrets Of Healthy Relationships
109. Ancestral Ties
110. The Indian Street Food
111. Discovering America
112. The Indian Textile
113. Listening To Motivational Speeches
114. Taste Of India
115. A Cultural Journey Through Indian Nuptials
116. Motivational Quote For Change
117. Secret Strategies For Making Money
118. Secrets To Cultivate A Positive Mindset
119. A Tapestry Of Cultures: Exploring India From Kashmir To Kanyakumari
120. Achieving Your Dreams With Resilience: Secret Strategies For Overcoming Obstacles

CONTACT

DR. JAGADEESH PILLAI

MBA & PhD in Vedic Science

Four Times Guinness World Record Holder

Winner of Mahatma Gandhi Vishwa Shanti Puraskar and
Global Peace Ambassador

Gemology, Astro & Vastu Consultant - Spiritual Counselor

Consultant for designing World Record Ideas

Efficient Tarot Card Reader

9839093003

myrichindia@gmail.com

drjagadeeshpillai@facebook

drjagadeeshpillai@instagram

jagadeeshpillai@youtube

www. JAGADEESHPILLAI.com

౮

|| LOKAHA SAMASTHAHA SUKHINO BHAVANTU ||